The Sea Is Salty

and other questions
about the oceans

Anita Ganeri

KINGFISHER
NEW YORK

First published 1995 by Kingfisher
This edition published 2011 by Kingfisher

Distributed in the U.S. and Canada by Macmillan,
175 Fifth Ave., New York, NY 10010

Library of Congress Cataloging-in-Publication data
has been applied for.

ISBN 978-0-7534-6521-9 (PB)

Kingfisher books are available for special promotions and
premiums. For details contact: Special Markets Department,
Macmillan, 175 Fifth Ave., New York, NY 10010.

For more information, please visit www.kingfisherbooks.com

Printed in China
9 8 7 6 5 4 3 2
2TR/0911/WKT/UTD/140MA

Consultants: Michael Chinery, Keith Lye
Illustrations: Chris Forsey 4–5, 6–7, 14–15, 20–21, 28–29, 30–31;
    Ruby Green cover; Nick Harris (Virgil Pomfret Agency)
    8–9; Tony Kenyon (B.L. Kearley) all cartoons; Nicki Palin
    10–11, 18–19; Maurice Pledger (Bernard Thornton) 16–17,
    24–25; Bryan Poole 12–13, 22–23, 26–27.

CONTENTS

How big is the ocean?

The ocean is truly ENORMOUS! It covers more than twice as much of Earth as land does. In fact, it's made up of four oceans—the Pacific, the Atlantic, the Indian, and the Arctic. Although these all have different names, they flow into one another, making one huge world ocean.

Don't go for a swim in the Arctic Ocean. It's the coldest of the oceans, and for most of the year, it's covered in ice.

Which is the biggest ocean?

The Pacific is by far the biggest ocean in the world. It's larger than the other three oceans put together, and it's also much deeper. If you look at a globe, you'll see that the Pacific Ocean reaches halfway around the world.

These drops of water show the oceans in order of size.

Pacific

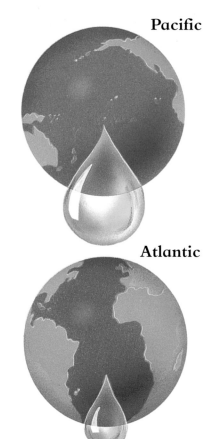

Atlantic

What's the difference between a sea and an ocean?

People often use the words *sea* and *ocean* to mean the same thing. That's fine, but to a scientist, seas are just part of an ocean—the parts that are closest to land. For example, the Caribbean Sea is between Central America and the Caribbean Islands.

Indian

Arctic

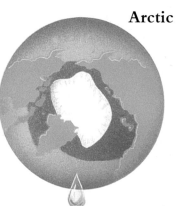

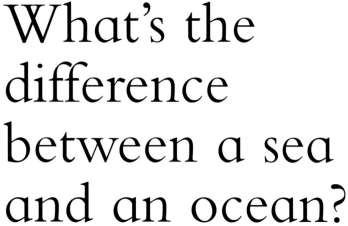

5

Why is the sea salty?

Seawater tastes salty because it has salt in it! The salt is the same as the stuff that people sprinkle on food. Most of it comes from rocks on land. Rain washes the salt into rivers, which carry it to the sea.

Most of Earth's water is salty. Only a tiny part is fresh water that we can drink.

Some of the sea salt that we use comes from hot places, such as India. People build low walls to trap the seawater when the tide comes in. When the sun dries up the water, the salt is left behind.

Is the Red Sea really red?

Some beaches around the Black Sea are covered with rich, dark mud. People spread it all over themselves—it's supposed to be good for the skin.

Parts of the Red Sea look red. During the summer, millions of tiny red plants called algae grow in the water. Don't worry— you won't turn pink if you swim there!

What did sailors fear the most?

Long ago, sailors had to put up with bad food, scary storms ... and pirate attacks! Pirates roamed the high seas, on the lookout for merchant ships loaded with fine goods and treasure. When the pirates found a ship, they boarded it, attacked the crew, and stole all the valuable goodies.

Blackbeard was one of the meanest pirates. To look extra fierce, he threaded rope through his beard and then set it on fire!

Real pirates didn't actually make people walk the plank. But the pirates you read about in stories often do!

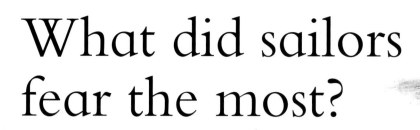

8

There weren't many female pirates. Anne Bonny and Mary Read are two of the most famous. They disguised themselves as men.

Who first sailed around the world?

In 1519, a fleet of five ships set off from Spain to sail around the world. Their captain, Ferdinand Magellan, was killed on the way. Only one ship and 18 men completed the journey. It took three years.

Times were tough for Magellan's men. When their food ran out, they had to eat grilled leather.

What is sand made of?

Not all sand is yellow. Some beaches have black, pinkish-white, or even green sand.

Look closely at a handful of sand and you'll see that it's made of tiny chips of rock and seashell. The pieces of rock come from cliffs that have been broken up by the rain and sea. The shells are washed in by the tide and crushed by the pounding waves.

Hang seaweed outside and it might forecast the weather! If it swells up, rain is on the way. If it dries out, the sun will shine.

Wreckers were people who shone lights to trick ships into crashing on rocks. Then they stole all the valuable things onboard and hid them in caves.

How are caves made?

As waves hurl sand and rocks against a cliff, the cliff is slowly worn away. The waves scoop out a small hollow and then a deep hole. After a very long time, the hole is worn into a dark, damp, and dripping cave.

You can often find empty seashells washed up on the seashore. Their owners have probably been eaten!

A tropical beach may look deserted, but dozens of different plants and animals make their homes there.

Why do limpets cling to rocks?

Like other animals on the seashore, limpets have tough lives. As the tide comes in, they are battered by the waves. As the tide goes out, they are tugged and pulled along by the swirling water. The poor limpets have to cling tightly onto rocks so that they aren't swept out to sea!

Which fish has a headlight?

It's so dark at the bottom of the ocean that some fish make their own light. The anglerfish has a long fin dangling in front of its face. At the end of the fin is a blob that glows. Small fish are drawn toward the glowing light, only to disappear into the anglerfish's big, gaping mouth.

The deep sea is inky black and as cold as a refrigerator. Even so, amazing creatures live there.

anglerfish

How deep is the ocean?

Away from the shore, the ocean plunges to about 2.5 miles (4km) in most places. That's deep enough to swallow ten Empire State Buildings stacked one on top of the other!

The seabed has huge cracks in it called trenches. Some are more than 6 miles (10km) deep.

What makes chimneys under the sea?

gulper eel

Fountains of boiling hot water gush out of holes in some parts of the seabed. Tiny grains sink down out of the hot water and form weird-looking chimney stacks around the holes.

Many deep-sea fish are kind of ugly. It's just as well that it's so dark down there!

Giant red-and-white worms as long as buses live around the chimneys.

dragonfish

What's it like at the bottom of the sea?

You might think that the bottom of the sea is smooth and flat, but it isn't—at least not everywhere. There are mountains and valleys, hills and plains, just as there are on land.

In 1963, a volcano erupted under the sea near Iceland. Hot, runny rock bubbled up to the surface of the water and hardened. It made a completely new island, which was named Surtsey.

Along the shore, the land slopes gently into the sea. This slope is called the continental shelf.

Flat plains cover one-half of the seabed. They are called abyssal plains.

The Mid-Atlantic Ridge is a long line of underwater mountains in the Atlantic Ocean.

Are there mountains under the sea?

There are earthquakes under the sea, just as there are on land. In fact, there are more than one million seaquakes each year! But most of them happen so deep down that we can't feel them.

Yes, many—and they are all volcanoes! Someone has counted about 10,000 of them, but there may be double this number. The scientific name for them is seamounts. Some are so high that they stick out of the water and make islands.

A trench is a deep valley in the seabed.

A seamount is an underwater volcano. There's a seamount erupting somewhere as you read this!

How do fish breathe underwater?

Fish have to breathe to stay alive, just as you do. But while you breathe oxygen from the air, fish get oxygen from water. As they swim, fish gulp in water and push it out through slits called gills on their heads. Oxygen passes from the water into the fish's blood inside their gills.

gill cover

Not all sea creatures can breathe underwater. Sea cows, seals, and dolphins breathe air, so they have to keep coming up to the surface.

How do fish swim?

Fish swim by using their muscles to ripple their bodies along. Wiggling their tails from side to side gives them extra push. They use their other fins to balance and change direction.

Which bird flies underwater?

Penguins can't fly through the air because their wings are too short and stumpy. They are much more at home in the ocean, where they use their wings as flippers.

Sea horses are not strong swimmers. They hang onto seaweed to avoid being swept away.

Which animal is jet-propelled?

Squids don't have flippers or a tail, but they're still fast movers. They suck water into their bodies and then squirt it out so powerfully that their bodies shoot backward.

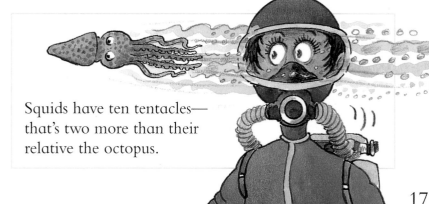

Squids have ten tentacles—that's two more than their relative the octopus.

Which animal loves to play?

Dolphins are playful and trusting. Some are so friendly that they will let you swim with them. Dolphins have even rescued drowning people, using their noses to nudge them to shore.

How do whales and dolphins use sound to see?

Whales and dolphins use their ears, not their eyes, to find their way around. As they swim, they make clicking noises that travel through the water. When the clicks hit something solid, an echo bounces back—just like a ball bouncing off a wall. The echo tells the animals what lies ahead.

Dolphins have up to 200 sharp, pointed teeth for holding onto slippery fish. Imagine brushing those every night!

Narwhals are a kind of whale with a very long tusk. Sailors used to sell narwhal tusks, pretending they were the horns of unicorns!

Which sea animals sing like birds?

White beluga whales are nicknamed "sea canaries" because they cheep and chirp like birds. They can also moo like cows, chime like bells, or press their lips together in a loud smack!

What makes waves roll?

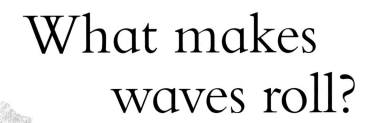

You can make your own waves in a bowl of water. The harder you blow across the surface, the bigger the waves will be.

Waves are ripples of water blown across the surface of the ocean by the wind. On a calm day, they hardly move, but in stormy weather, they roll faster and faster and grow higher and higher, until they form huge walls of water.

Some waves are called white horses because their curly white tips look like horses' manes.

At Waimea Bay, Hawaii, surfers ride waves up to 33 ft. (10m) high—that's six times taller than an adult!

Palm trees can grow in a chilly place like Scotland because warm currents flow along the west coast, bringing water from much hotter parts of the world.

Are there rivers in the ocean?

The ocean has large bands of water called currents that flow like rivers. They travel faster than the water around them, moving from one part of the world to another.

Ocean currents can carry a message in a bottle for you. But don't expect fast service. One floated for 73 years before it was washed up!

Why do sailors watch the tide?

In Canada's Bay of Fundy, the water at high tide is about 50 feet (15m) deeper than at low tide—that's the height of a five-story house!

Twice a day, the sea comes high up on the beach and then goes back again. At high tide, the water is deep, and sailboats can sail in and out of a harbor. But at low tide, the water is so shallow that sailors are either stuck on the shore or out at sea!

Where do angels, clowns, and parrots live?

Angelfish, clown fish, and parrotfish are just some of the thousands of beautiful animals that live on coral reefs. Tropical fish like these often have dazzling colors and bold patterns.

Coral reefs grow in shallow water in the warmest parts of the world.

imperial angelfish

parrotfish

angelfish

Giant clams live on coral reefs. Their shells are big enough to take a bath in!

What is a coral reef?

Corals come in all sorts of shapes—antlers, plates, mushrooms, feathers, daisies, and even brains!

A coral reef is like a beautiful underwater hedge. It looks stony and dead—but it is actually alive! Coral is made up of millions of tiny animals that leave their hard skeletons behind when they die. Each new layer piles on top of the old one, slowly building the coral rock.

Where is the biggest reef?

The world's biggest coral reef lies in the warm shallow sea off the northeast coast of Australia. It is called the Great Barrier Reef, and it stretches for more than 1,240 miles (2,000km). It's so huge that it can be seen by astronauts up in space.

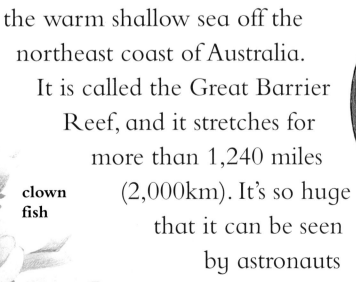

clown fish

23

Which is the biggest fish?

The dwarf goby is the smallest fish in the ocean.

The whale shark is the world's biggest fish. It's gigantic—as long as eight scuba divers lying head to toe and as heavy as six large elephants.

The oarfish is the longest fish in the ocean—as long as four canoes placed end to end.

oarfish

sailfish

The biggest sea plant is the giant kelp seaweed. A single strand can grow almost as long as a soccer field!

Which is the fastest fish?

The sailfish can race along underwater at more than 60 mph (100km/h)—as fast as a car. It tucks its fins in tightly, and its pointed nose cuts through the water like a knife.

whale shark

Which is the biggest crab?

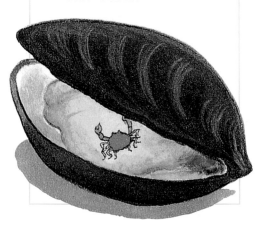

The pea-size pea crab is the smallest crab of all. It lives inside oyster and mussel shells.

Japan's giant spider crab measures almost 13 feet (4m) from the tip of one claw to the tip of the other. It can open its arms wide enough to hug a hippopotamus!

Which fish hunts with a hammer?

The hammerhead shark has a huge head shaped like a hammer. But this tool is for hunting, not banging on nails. The shark's eyes and nostrils are at each end of the hammer. As the shark swims, it swings its head from side to side, searching for a meal.

Which is the most shocking fish?

The Portuguese man-of-war catches its food in its long, stinging tentacles.

Some fish give off electric shocks to protect themselves or to stun animals that they want to eat. The most shocking ocean fish is the torpedo ray. If you could turn it on, it would light up a light bulb!

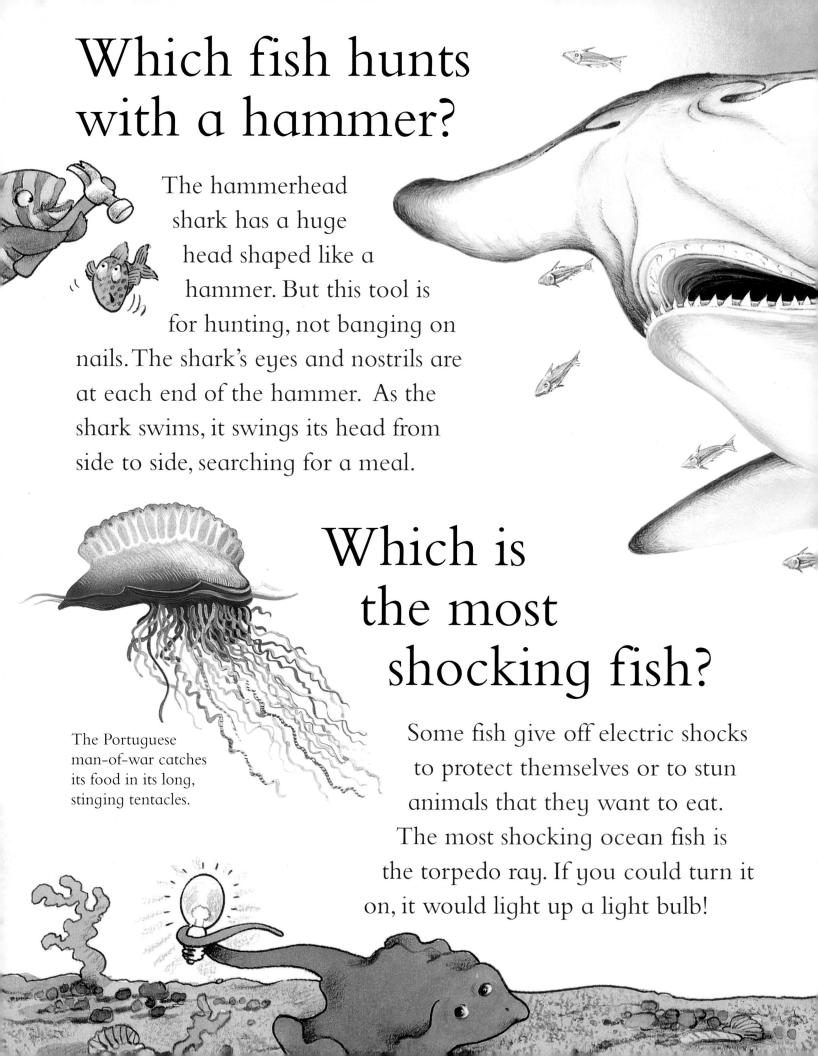

Thousands of mackerel swim together in one huge school. Their enemies find it difficult to pick out a single fish from the shimmering silvery mass.

Which fish look like stones?

Stonefish look just like lumps of rock—but they're much more dangerous. If attacked, a stonefish uses the needle-sharp spines on its fins to stab its enemy with a deadly poison.

The leafy sea dragon looks just like a ragged strand of seaweed. What a perfect disguise!

How deep can submarines dive?

Few submarines can dive much lower than 660 ft. (200m) below the surface of the ocean. That's about 100 times deeper than an Olympic-size swimming pool.

What dives the deepest?

Divers use smaller craft called submersibles to explore deep water and to look for wrecks and sunken treasure. The *Titanic* was an enormous ocean liner that sank around 100 years ago. Divers discovered the wreck, 12,405 feet (3,781m) down, in 1985. They were able to reach it in a submersible called *Alvin*.

The *Titanic* was launched in 1912. On its first voyage, it hit an iceberg and sank in the Atlantic Ocean.

Which was the deepest dive ever?

In 1960, two men dived almost 7 miles (11km) into the Marianas Trench in the Pacific Ocean. They were inside one of the first submersibles, an incredibly strong craft called *Trieste*. The submersible took about five hours to reach the bottom.

Divers wear special suits of armor in deep water. This one is called *Spider*. It's like a one-person submarine!

In the deepest parts of the ocean, the water presses down so hard that to be there would be like having ten elephants sitting on top of you!

Who fishes with fire?

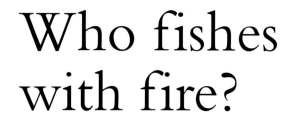

On an island in the Pacific Ocean, people fish in the darkness of night. They set fire to the branches of coconut trees and then hang them over the sides of their boats. The fish swim toward the firelight—only to be caught by the islanders' sharp spears.

Seaweed is rich in nutrients, so farmers spread it on their land to improve the soil. It is also used to thicken ice cream and toothpaste.

Are there farms under the sea?

Yes, but there aren't any farmers, cows, or sheep! Some kinds of fish and shellfish are raised in large cages out at sea. The fish are so well fed that they grow much more quickly than they would in the wild.

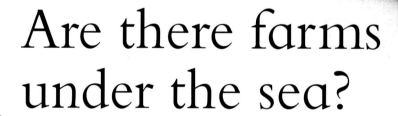

People all around the world have different legends that tell how Earth was created. Some say that it was made inside a giant clamshell. It must have been *some* shell!

Are there jewels in the sea?

In warm tropical water, pearls may grow inside the shells of oysters and clams. The pearls are such rare finds that they are very valuable. People risk their lives diving down for them.

The biggest pearl ever found was as large as your head. Imagine wearing it around your neck!

Index